The Science of the
Environment

LIVINGSCIENCE

Patricia Miller-Schroeder

Gareth Stevens Publishing
A WORLD ALMANAC EDUCATION GROUP COMPANY

Please visit our web site at: www.garethstevens.com
For a free color catalog describing Gareth Stevens' list of high-quality books and
multimedia programs, call 1-800-542-2595 (USA) or 1-800-461-9120 (Canada).
Gareth Stevens Publishing's Fax: (414) 332-3567.

Library of Congress Cataloging-in-Publication Data

Miller-Schroeder, Patricia.
    The science of the environment / by Patricia Miller-Schroeder.
      p. cm. – (Living science)
    Includes index.
    ISBN 0-8368-2788-0 (lib. bdg.)
    1. Environmental sciences–Juvenile literature. [1. Environmental sciences.] I. Title.
  II. Living science (Milwaukee, Wis.)
  GE115 .M55   2001
  333.95–dc21   00-063755

This edition first published in 2001 by
Gareth Stevens Publishing
A World Almanac Education Group Company
330 West Olive Street, Suite 100
Milwaukee, WI 53212 USA

Project Co-ordinator: Jared Keen
Series Editor: Celeste Peters
Copy Editor: Heather Kissock
Design: Warren Clark
Cover Design: Terry Paulhus
Layout: Lucinda Cage
Gareth Stevens Editor: Jean B. Black

Every reasonable effort has been made to trace ownership and to obtain permission to reprint
copyright material. The publishers would be pleased to have any errors or omissions brought
to their attention so that they may be corrected in subsequent printings.

Photograph Credits:
Corel Corporation: cover, pages 5 left, 5 top right, 6 left, 7 center, 7 bottom, 8, 9, 10 bottom, 11 top,
12 bottom, 13, 14, 15, 16 bottom, 18, 19, 20, 21, 23, 24, 29 top left, 29 top right; Digital Vision:
pages 25, 30; Lloyd Harris: page 4; PhotoDisc: page 28; Tom Stack & Associates: pages 10 top
(W. Perry Conway), 17 top (Brian Parker), 22 top left (Kevin Magee), 27 top (Inga Spence), 27
bottom (Joanne Lotter), 31 (Dave Watts); Monique de St. Croix: pages 5 bottom right, 6 right, 7 top,
22 bottom left; Visuals Unlimited: pages 11 bottom (Jane Thomas), 12 top (C.P. George), 16 top
(John D. Cunningham), 17 bottom (Johnathan D. Speer), 22 top right (William Grenfell), 22
bottom right (Hugh Rose), 26 (D. Cavagnaro), 29 bottom left, 29 bottom right (Ken Lucas).

Printed in the United States of America

1 2 3 4 5 6 7 8 9 05 04 03 02 01

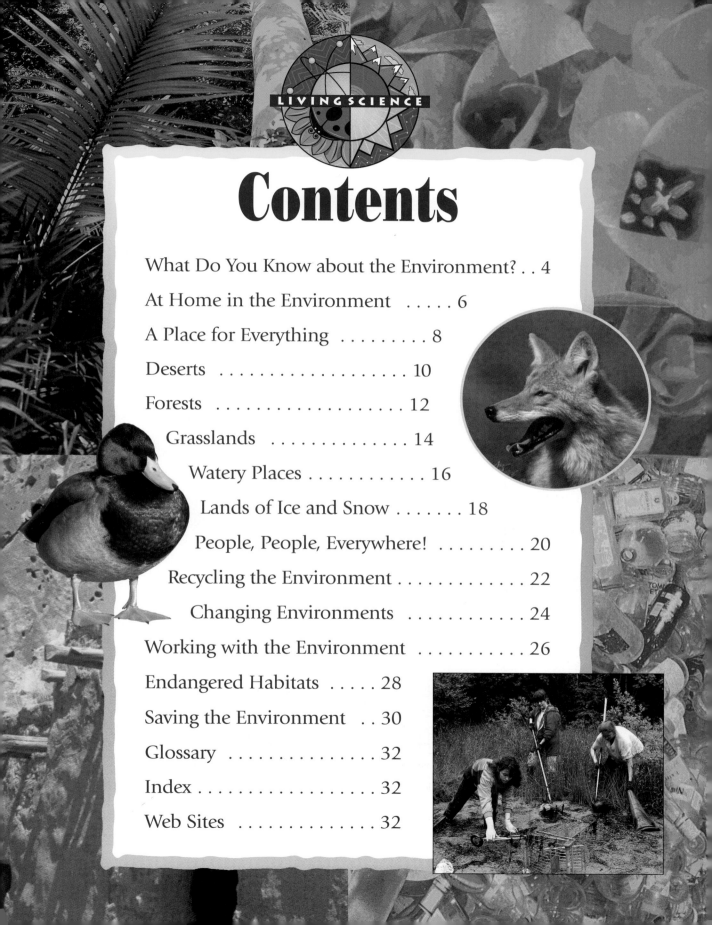

Contents

What Do You Know about the Environment?

Wherever you are right now, stop and look around you. Everything you see and many things you do not see make up your **environment**. You might be in the same place two hours from now. You might be in your bedroom, at school, or at the playground. Wherever you are, you are in your environment!

The environment is a person's or an animal's surroundings. An ant's environment could be a flower or a backyard lawn.

The environment is everything around us, wherever we go. It is all of the plants, animals, people, soil, air, water, and energies that surround us. Things that are built, such as houses, furniture, cars, roads, and fences, are part of the environment, too.

People share the environment with many other people, plants, and animals. Everyone depends on it for their health and well-being. That is why taking care of the environment is important. If people are not careful, the things they do to the environment will damage it.

Trees are an important part of a bird's environment.

Activity

List It!

Choose your favorite environment. It might be your bedroom, the garden, or someplace else. Make a list of all the things you see in this environment.

A playground can be a fun part of your environment.

At Home in the Environment

The part of the environment in which an animal lives is called its **habitat**. This place is the animal's home. A habitat must provide certain things to keep an animal alive.

Fresh Water
keeps an animal's body working properly. Most animals cannot survive very long without clean drinking water.

Food
is the fuel that keeps an animal going. Most animals eat only a few types of food. These foods must be present in their habitats.

Shelter
protects an animal from heat, cold, and storms. It also gives animals a safe place to hide from **predators**.

Air
provides the oxygen an animal needs to stay alive. Most animals cannot survive without fresh, clean air to breathe.

Puzzler
Does a fish need air in its habitat?

Answer: Yes. All living things need air to live. A fish gets its air from water.

Space
gives an animal room to move around. Animals need space in which to find food and **reproduce**.

A Place for Everything

Can an octopus live at the North Pole? Not for long! An octopus does not belong in a polar **ecosystem**. Earth has several types of ecosystems, called biomes. Each biome contains different plants, animals, and habitats.

Biomes

Deserts	Forests	Grasslands

• usually hot during the day • very dry • plants store water to survive	• plenty of freshwater • the most common plants are trees • animals live in and under trees	• large, open areas • ground is covered with grasses • many grazing animals

Examples

Death Valley, Gobi Desert, Sahara Desert	**Brazilian rain forest, pine forests of North America**	**Great Plains of North America, Serengeti Plains of Africa**

Puzzler

In which biome would each of the following animals live?

- a blue whale
- a camel
- a black bear
- a zebra

Wetlands	Oceans and Seas	Polar Regions

• marshes, swamps, rivers, and lakeshores • provide shelter and food for nesting birds and other small animals	• large bodies of saltwater • the most common animals are fish • many underwater plants	• very long days in summer • very long nights in winter • very cold • no trees
Florida Everglades, Mississippi River delta	**Indian Ocean, Pacific Ocean, Mediterranean Sea**	**Canadian Arctic, Antarctica**

Deserts

Deserts are dry places that get very little rain. At times, no rain falls for months or even years. Most deserts are very hot, but cold deserts can be found near the North and South Poles. Although deserts look bare from a distance, they are home to many plants and animals.

Plants and animals that live in deserts have **adapted** to the dry environment. Some plants, such as the cactus, store water inside of them. Other plants have bulbs or seeds that stay alive a long time between rains.

Some desert animals, such as the fennec fox, have large ears. Heat escapes through the ears, keeping the animals cool.

Deserts get less than 10 inches (250 millimeters) of rain each year.

Many desert animals sleep in underground holes while the day is hot. They come out at night, when the air is cooler. Desert animals do not need to drink much water. Some drink none at all! Instead, they get their water from their food. Camels can go a long time without drinking water. During this time, they survive on water that is stored in their body fat.

The addax is an African antelope that lives most of its life without drinking. It gets water from the plants it eats.

The Sahara Desert in northern Africa is the largest desert in the world. It covers 3.5 million square miles (9 million square kilometers).

Puzzler

After a rain, the bare desert seems to burst with colorful plants. They grow almost overnight. How does this sudden growth happen?

Answer: The desert soil is full of plant seeds and bulbs. When rain falls, they start growing very quickly.

Forests

Earth's forests provide homes for millions of living things. In fact, more than half of all the different kinds of plants and animals live in **tropical** rain forests. Sometimes these forests are called jungles. They are very wet places.

Trees are the most common plants in rain forests. Ferns, mosses, vines, and orchids also grow there. Animals live everywhere, from beneath the ground right up to the treetops. Many foods and medicines come from rain forests, too.

Gorillas usually travel and eat on the rain forest floor.

Parrots eat fruits, nuts, seeds, and buds found in rain forests.

Forests also grow in colder parts of the world. Some of these forests have **deciduous** trees, including maple and birch. Deciduous trees lose their leaves in autumn. The leaves that fall to the ground make the soil rich. They also provide shelter for insects and other small animals. Deciduous trees grow new leaves in spring.

In some forests, the trees are evergreens, such as spruce and pine. Many evergreens are **coniferous** trees. Instead of leaves, they have needles, which they keep all year long.

The rain forest is home to a wide variety of animals and plants, including spiders, snakes, and orchids.

Which of these things come from forests?

- bananas
- coconuts
- lumber
- paper
- maple syrup
- rubber

Answer: Forests provide all of these things.

Grasslands

Wind blows across wide, open spaces. Wild grasses cover huge plots of ground. Blue sky stretches overhead. Welcome to the grasslands! Grasslands are found on every continent except Antarctica. They are a major source of food for humans and many other animals.

The wild grasses that grow on grasslands are tough. They have adapted to heat, cold, fires, and low rainfall. People often plant grains on grasslands. These crops are not as tough as the wild grasses and need special care to grow.

Burrowing owls nest in grasslands.

Wheat covers more of Earth than any other food crop.

14

Many creatures live on grasslands. Some graze on the grasses and other plants that grow there. Mice and other rodents burrow under the ground. Predators, such as foxes, lions, and hawks, hunt other grassland animals.

People often dig up grasslands. They use the land for growing crops and feeding livestock. Sometimes, they do not leave much room for wildlife.

Zebras live on the grasslands of Africa.

Puzzler

How do seeds spread?

Answer:
The movements of wind, water, birds, and mammals help spread seeds.

Coyotes live in many different environments. They can be found in grassland, desert, and mountain areas.

Prairie dogs live on the grasslands of western North America.

15

Watery Places

More plants and animals live in water than on land. This fact should not be surprising, since oceans and wetlands cover nearly three-fourths of Earth's surface. Wetlands include ponds, marshes, swamps, rivers, and lakeshores.

The world's largest living creature is the blue whale. It lives in the ocean. So do tiny plants and animals called **plankton**. Plankton are too small to see with human eyes alone. Some wetland creatures, such as frogs, spend part of their lives on land and part in water. Many birds stop at wetlands to feed and nest.

Fish have fins to help them swim through water.

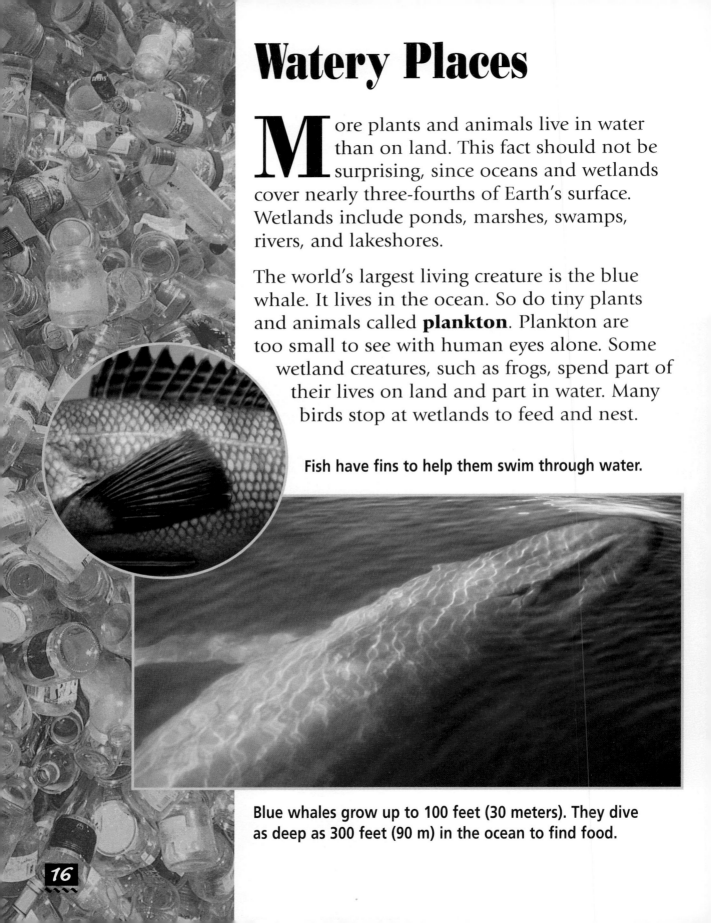

Blue whales grow up to 100 feet (30 meters). They dive as deep as 300 feet (90 m) in the ocean to find food.

Many animals have adapted to life in watery places. Fish have gills and fins to help them breathe and swim underwater. Animals such as beavers and crocodiles have webbed feet to help them swim. The feet of seals and sea turtles are flippers that look and work like paddles. Plants also have adapted to life in the water. Some plants in shallow water have roots to hold them in place. Other plants float on or in the water.

Activity

Aquarium Safari

Visit a public aquarium. Take a camera with you. Find and take photos of the following:

- coral
- an octopus
- a seal
- a shark
- a large fish
- a tiny fish
- a whale

Place your photos in an album to make a nice souvenir of your trip to the aquarium!

Mangrove trees often grow beside lagoons, bays, and rivers. Some grow in salty ocean water.

Ducks spend most of their time in water. Their webbed feet help them swim.

17

Lands of Ice and Snow

Could you live where it is cold all year long and dark for months at a time? Some plants and animals can. They have adapted to life on the **Arctic tundra**.

The Arctic tundra is a flat area near the Arctic Ocean where it is too cold for trees to grow. The ground below the surface soil is always frozen. The plants that grow on the tundra are very short. Berry bushes grow in patches hugging the ground. Tundra plants must grow quickly. The Sun shines there during only half of the year.

The fur of the Arctic fox turns white in winter. Having fur the color of snow helps the fox hide from predators.

In winter, snowy owls move south from the Arctic. Some fly all the way to the Gulf of Mexico!

In spring, biting flies and mosquitoes hatch in swarms. Thousands of ducks and geese fly in to feed on these insects and to nest. Large animals, such as musk oxen and caribou, eat Arctic plants. These animals, in turn, are eaten by wolves. Polar bears hunt seals that live on the polar ice. Arctic foxes eat whatever they can find, dead or alive.

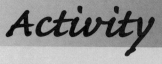

Activity

Coping with the Cold
Look carefully at the pictures of the Arctic fox, snowy owl, polar bear, and musk oxen on these pages. What features do these animals have that help them live in a cold environment? Make a list.

Most polar bears live where the sea ice surrounding the North Pole breaks up. These bears are found in Canada, Greenland, Russia, and on islands in the Arctic Ocean.

Musk oxen have the longest hair of any animal. Their hair helps them survive in their cold environment.

People, People, Everywhere!

Most plants and animals have adapted to life in only one biome. They have a difficult time living outside it. For example, polar bears cannot live in deserts or on grasslands. Humans, on the other hand, live in every biome on Earth. How? Humans can make and build things that help them survive. They can adapt to different environments.

The Inuit, formerly known as Eskimos, live in some of the harshest environments in the world. Few plants and animals can live as far north as these Native people do.

The first people to live in very cold places made warm clothes from the skins and furs of animals. They also built shelters, such as igloos, to keep themselves warm. They learned to travel over the snow with dogsleds and snowshoes.

People have learned to build shelters in many other places, too. Where it is very warm, they leave openings in the shelter walls to let breezes blow through. In areas that flood, they build shelters on stilts to keep them above the water when it rises. Humans also build shelters in which many people can live close together on a small piece of land.

Apartment buildings house many people in one space.

Huts (above) help keep people cool in hot areas. The cliff houses (left) built by Native Americans protected them from enemy attacks.

Puzzler

People often move to new environments. Do you know where some people are trying to move now?

Answer:
People are trying to move into outer space. Some astronauts now live in space stations for over a hundred days at a time. People are also looking at ways to live on the Moon and on the planet Mars.

Recycling the Environment

Nothing is wasted in the natural environment. Everything is **recycled**, or reused, keeping the environment healthy. Food cycles show how natural recycling works.

Plants are eaten by animals called **herbivores**. Those animals are often eaten by animals called **carnivores**. The remains of dead plants and animals keep the soil rich to grow new plants. These plants are then eaten, and the food cycle continues.

Many cycles depend on one another. The food cycle, for example, depends on the water cycle. Plants and animals need water to live and grow.

How do plants and animals get water? Moisture from the oceans gathers into clouds and then falls as rain or snow. Water from rain and snow flows in rivers and streams both above and below ground. Animals drink water from lakes and rivers. Plants absorb water through their roots. Water that is not used by plants or animals flows back to the oceans.

Many plants and animals rely on clouds for water. Rain and snow fall from the clouds and form streams, rivers, and lakes.

Changing Environments

An environment can change naturally over time. Changes happen, for example, when beavers build a dam on a stream. The dam floods nearby areas, and some plants and animals must move out or die. Other animals who live well in flooded areas move in. These changes happen slowly and naturally.

Beavers use their sharp teeth to cut down trees for their dams and lodges. Lodges are their homes in the water.

People sometimes cause sudden changes in the environment. When people chop down trees in a forest, they change that environment. Some plants and animals might not be able to live there anymore. With no tree roots left to hold it in place, the forest soil washes away with the rain. Any soil that is left offers little food for plants, so crops and trees will not grow very well.

People and trees need each other to live. People breathe in oxygen from the air and breathe out **carbon dioxide**. Trees take in carbon dioxide and release oxygen. When there is too much carbon dioxide in the air, trees help remove it. Trees that are cut down can no longer help.

Humans use trees to build houses and furniture and to make paper and many other products.

Activity

Add Some Greenery
Ask a parent or a teacher to help you plant a tree. Now you are helping trees help the environment.

Bulldozers can change environments, too. People use them to clear trees to make room for roads and buildings.

Working with the Environment

Would you like to work with the environment? Many people do. **Biologists**, for example, study living things and how they relate to one another. People go to universities or colleges to become biologists. Some biologists work for governments or for universities. Others work for museums, zoos, aquariums, or even private companies.

Biologists who study certain kinds of living things have special names. Biologists who study plants are botanists. Those who study animals are zoologists. Biologists who study living things in their natural habitats are called ecologists.

Botanists work closely with plants. Some collect samples from forest floors and treetops. Others study plants they grow from seeds.

Wildlife resource officers work in national parks. They are often called "park rangers." They protect wildlife and their habitats. Park rangers make sure people obey the rules. They watch for anyone who might be harming wildlife or the environment. Rangers try to make sure both wildlife and people are safe.

Activity

Do Your Own Research

Ask a parent or a teacher to help you find information about these careers:

- botanist
- ecologist
- environmental educator
- environmental engineer
- environmental lawyer
- organic farmer
- urban planner
- weather forecaster
- zoologist

Some biologists study birds by putting bands on them. The bands help scientists track the birds to learn more about them.

Environmental educators teach people about the wonders of the natural world.

Endangered Habitats

People share the environment with all other living things, but the number of people is growing. By the year 2050, there will probably be 10 billion people on Earth. As people use more of Earth's resources, they leave fewer habitats for plants and animals. People also create **pollution**. Pollution destroys habitats, too.

Some of the most endangered habitats are rain forests.

As people build homes and cities, natural habitats shrink. Shrinking habitats cannot support all the creatures that live in them. Some plants and animals must move or die. Many are endangered. Some even become **extinct**. They disappear forever.

Certain animals warn us when a habitat is in trouble from pollution. They are the first to disappear from the habitat if something is wrong. Dragonflies and many types of frogs are good examples of these animals.

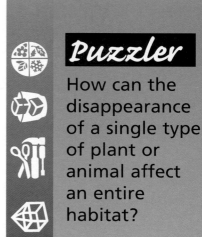

Puzzler

How can the disappearance of a single type of plant or animal affect an entire habitat?

Answer: Many animals require the same food sources. When even a single food source vanishes, many kinds of animals might be left without enough to eat.

mountain gorilla

Siberian tiger

black-footed ferret

golden lion tamarin

Many animals are vanishing from Earth. As their habitats are destroyed, they can no longer survive.

Saving the Environment

Today, many people are working to save the environment. Some are members of groups, such as Friends of the Earth and the World Wildlife Fund. These groups work to save endangered plants, animals, and habitats. You can join one of these groups and help them.

Your class at school can also take on projects to help save the environment. Maybe your whole school can become a green school. A green school helps prevent pollution. It reuses, recycles, and reduces its supplies.

There are many ways to help preserve the environment. Some people clear away garbage from natural areas, including forests and ponds.

You can help prevent pollution. Get your family and your class at school involved in the three Rs:

Recycle: Collect used newspapers, paper, cardboard, cans, bottles, and plastic containers to be recycled. Recycling turns used materials into new products. You can recycle kitchen and yard wastes, too. Put them in a compost bin to make new soil.

Reuse: Reuse things you would normally throw out. Use your imagination. See what you can create.

Reduce: Reduce the amount of packaging you use. Take your lunch to school in reusable containers. Carry your own reusable bags when you go shopping. Do not buy things that have too much packaging. You can make a difference!

Environmentalists plant trees and other plants to replace those that are cut down or destroyed.

Glossary

adapted: changed to suit the environment.

Arctic tundra: cold, treeless land near the Arctic Ocean.

biologists: scientists who study living things.

carbon dioxide: a gas that plants take in.

carnivores: animals that eat meat.

compost: a mixture of dead plants and other waste material that turns into soil.

coniferous: having needles and cones.

deciduous: shedding leaves each year.

ecosystem: a community of plants and animals.

endangered: in danger of becoming extinct.

environment: everything in a plant's or animal's surroundings.

extinct: none left in the world.

habitat: the place in an environment where an animal lives.

herbivores: animals that eat plants.

oxygen: a gas that animals breathe.

plankton: very tiny plants and animals that live in oceans.

pollution: any material put where it can harm the environment.

predators: animals that hunt and eat other animals.

recycled: used again.

reproduce: create babies.

tropical: related to the hot, moist regions near the equator.

Index

Web Sites

tqjunior.thinkquest.org/6076/

www.earth2kids.org

www.nwf.org/nwf/kids/

www.worldwildlife.org/fun/kids.cfm

Some web sites stay current longer than others. For further web sites, use your search engines to locate the following topics: *ecology, ecosystem, environment, habitat,* and *wildlife.*

DATE DUE
